MOTHER ALSO SAID

Also by Isha Mellor
My Mother Said

ISHA MELLOR

MOTHER
ALSO SAID

ILLUSTRATED BY
RODNEY SHACKELL

W. H. ALLEN · LONDON

A Howard & Wyndham Company

1979

Printed and bound in Great Britain by
W & J Mackay Limited, Chatham
for the Publishers, W. H. Allen & Co. Ltd,
44 Hill Street, London W1X 8LB

ISBN 0 491 02079 1

CONTENTS

INTRODUCTION

The response to *My Mother Said* has been so enthusi-
astic that I have been encouraged to delve once more
into memories of how things used to be done in my
family, and to produce a further collection of idio-
syncratic advice.

It has been particularly interesting to learn that men
have enjoyed reading the book and been reluctant to
put it down. It seems they were intrigued by all the
sections – not only the handyman hints – so there may
in future be much more equality of work within the
home.

I have met readers who have declared, 'I tried it,
and it works!' and gone on to describe for my use their
own special wrinkles. Some of these I have been
privileged to include in *Mother Also Said*.

PRACTICALITIES

Saving fingers

Like all little girls I was always playing with the button box, and of course I found a ring in it that just fitted on my finger. Panic set in when I couldn't get it off, and a jokey aunt said my finger would have to be cut off. But Mother had a solution:

She threaded a needle with strong thread, passed the head of the needle under the ring towards the wrist, and pulled one end of the thread a few inches through, discarding the needle. She then took the long end of the thread that lay in the opposite direction and wound it tightly and regularly round the finger as far as the nail. Taking hold of the short end, she began to unwind that. Magically, this action began to urge the ring upwards, and I was released, sure of remaining attached to my finger.

Dust in the eyes

Before using an electric drill to make holes in a ceiling, fit a plastic lid over the bit. This will catch the dust and save your eyes and hair from trouble. The lid should be steadied with one hand while operating.

Talcum powder

Talcum applied to tool handles will prevent blisters forming on tender skin not used to manual work.

Sticky playing cards can be rendered usable by having talcum worked into them. The first game should not be played when wearing dark clothes, of course.

Double action

A hint that provides two benefits is always satisfactory. It is almost impossible to pour oil from a bottle without a small trickle running down to form an obstinate stickiness on the shelf. Adopt the habit of wiping the bottle itself against the back of the hand. The bottle is thus cleaned, and the skin benefits from the slight lubrication.

Party cubes

In order to have enough ice for party drinks, start making them a few days in advance and storing them in a polythene bag. A sharp knock of the bag on the floor will separate the cubes most efficiently.

Stop that row

My baby son was enjoying a fit of screaming and crying the day we visited Grandma. Nothing would stop him. But it really did seem to be an excessive reaction when I saw her leave the room and presently return with a heavy hammer. I clutched my child protectively. She merely gave one sharp bang on the floor – and there was instant silence. After stopping to consider this competition, baby then forgot what he had been making a fuss about.

Shore lore

Little pebbles collected from the shore, boiled clean and stored, make a good substitute for beans to weight down pastry cases that have to be baked blind. The more usual beans are far too expensive to use in this way.

Larger pebbles arranged over the earth round pot plants look very pleasant and also help to delay drying out.

Precious stuff

Amber: Never wash it, but rub gently with soft duster. Keep it away from hair sprays and perfume. Since amber has a tranquillizing effect when handled, the stones make excellent worry beads. Said also to be good against sore throats and asthma.

Gold: Brush ornate jewellery with very soft brush. Otherwise, it can be washed in warm suds containing 10–15 drops of *sal volatile* – the stuff Victorian ladies took for the vapours.

Jade: Wash from time to time in warm water and soap flakes. Handle as much as possible. The Chinese used to take powdered jade as a cure for 'pain in the side' which sounds vague, and Walter Raleigh reported it as being used for renal diseases. Test for genuineness by dropping a little water onto it. Water will not run off real jade. I was once nearly doused by an enthusiast trying this out on my green pendant that was not jade.

Pearl: Real and cultured pearls feel gritty when rubbed against one's front teeth or across the biting edge – without biting.

Suspicions

An old bishop was convinced that his servants were helping themselves out of his lidded sugar bowl. So he caught a fly and trapped it in the bowl. When next he looked, if the fly was flown, he knew he could rightly accuse his wretched staff of pinching his sugar lumps. It must have been good to be a fly in his house!

Another person with a suspicious nature used to fasten a hair from the drawer handle of a chest to the handle of the drawer above. In this way he could tell if anyone had been to the drawers he had thus booby-trapped.

Pests

She was such a sweet and gentle old lady who told me of this way of keeping mice away. 'First,' she said with utter reasonableness, 'you cremate the body of a mouse, and then sprinkle the ashes near the mouse holes. This protection will last for up to two years,' she assured me. When I asked how one might cremate a mouse, she said, 'Well, you can put the body in a cocoa tin and place the tin on the fire.' A thoroughly nasty and maybe dangerous system, but one can get really desperate when plagued with mice.

I have had success when baiting traps with chocolate, and as mice are supposed to love peppermint, after-dinner mints will surely tempt the discerning creatures.

Strips of cucumber peel placed by cracks in the skirting will ward off invasion by beetles. And cock-roaches can be got rid of by placing icing sugar mixed with equal quantities of borax near the places where they emerge at night. They love the sugar and do not notice the borax which is very bad for them.

Draught excluder

The very thin polythene clothes covers from dry-cleaning shops can be unobtrusively used for the problem of draught-proofing ill-fitted sash windows. Squeeze the covers into rope-like lengths and force them into the cracks, using something like a paper-knife to ram them home. This treatment is for windows that one does not propose to open during the winter.

Mirror mirror

Black spots on mirrors, caused by the silvering begin-
ning to break up, may be disguised for a while by
taping shiny silver foil over the area. Naturally, the
tape must not be peeled off once on, or more damage
will be caused. This remedy will serve until the pro-
fessionals take over the job of re-silvering.

Paint stripping

When dealing with vertical surfaces, a good method to
adopt that will prevent nasty trickles down to one's
elbow is to apply the caustic agent to wallpaper paste.
This adheres well with no drips. It should be washed
off before the paste dries.

Stocking top

When a pot of paint develops bits of skin that get into the brush and then onto one's beautiful new surfaces, look for an old pair of tights and secure a piece from them loosely over the top of the tin so that it sags into the paint. The brush can then be dipped into the strained pool of paint.

Double knot

'It's not right, you know.' That was the disconcerting comment from my know-all friend as he watched me tying string geometrically in neat squares round a parcel for posting. 'The Post Office like you to tie a parcel with one piece of string and then cross it with another separate piece. You must get two independent sets of knots.' Sensible, really, because one long string could become completely unravelled.

Spelling out thrift

It takes guts to tear up and burn the typescript of a first novel that after twenty or more rejections lies collecting dust. A now successful novelist told me that he typed the first draft of another book on the back of the pages of an early failure. In so doing he came across sections that he was able to use again, and he developed quite a respect for that younger author.

Personal columns

The older one becomes the more it is essential to read the hatched, matched, and despatched columns. But nowadays, with fewer and fewer national newspapers, these columns have become far too long to digest properly. A most efficient couple have decided to share the task. The husband reads from A to K, and the wife from L to Z.

Good pull up

When the cords of curtain tapes have been drawn up to make the gathers, the surplus has an untidy habit of dangling in full view at the edges of the curtains. It is a good idea to draw them up from the centre – having firmly knotted them at each end, of course. A single knot and bow in the middle is quite sufficient, and easy to untie before laundering. The gathering process is also simpler to control if done in this way.

Anti-freeze

In primitive areas where water has to be pumped, it is useful to know that if the handle of the pump is left high before one goes to bed it will not be frozen and jammed in the morning when one desperately needs a hot cup of tea.

Leftover paint

This forms huge and wasteful skins when left in the bottom of nearly empty tins. It is best poured into small screw top jars for use at a later date. But do label them clearly. It can be disconcerting to grab a jar of mayonnaise only to find it contains creamy paint.

HEALTH
AND
BEAUTY

Non-smoker

When anti-social visitors have made your room un-
healthy with cigarette smoke, the smell may be dis-
pelled quite simply if you light an ordinary candle and
let it stay for half an hour or so.

Sick baby

A baby that has to lie in its cot while ill can be kept
quietly amused if crumpled paper is scattered over the
covers at the end of the cot. Every time the baby kicks,

the rustling caused will keep it intrigued and happy. A watch should be kept to see that the paper stays away from hands and mouth.

Private treatment

Most mothers find worms a distressing affliction when visited on their children, so they may be glad to hear of a cure that can do the trick in private. Rub a hard crust of bread with olive oil, garlic and salt. Then persuade the victim to eat this.

Corn cures

A friend let me have a look into her most precious book – a little paperback of the late 19th century entitled *Mrs Lavender's Herbal Book* – and I specially liked the corn cure recommended:

Soak two or three ivy leaves in vinegar for at least twenty-four hours. Apply to corn with a bandage. Relief will be instantaneous, but a complete cure, when the corn will come away, may take up to a month of daily applications of freshly soaked leaves.

Or one may try applying a cut cranberry to a corn.

Warts

Mother swears that her childhood warts were cured by rubbing with raw chicken skin taken from the drumstick, every Sunday.

For a simpler method, apply the milky fluid from a dandelion stalk.

Chilblains

This permanent cure for chilblains sounds more like a sadist's indulgence, but my informant assures me that this treatment carried out on him was not all that bad. Whatever discomfort he did endure was well worth the freedom he has since enjoyed from this winter curse.

The afflicted toes have to be beaten with a sprig of

holly until the blackish blood springs out of the needle-like wounds. So far so good, because the sensation resembles that of the bliss that comes from a good scratch on itching flesh. The next stage in the treatment is for salt to be rubbed into the wounds and left on for twenty-four hours. That is the testing point. The itching and stinging is unbearable – almost, and few endure it for the full period. But even with a degree of cheating the result is quite wonderful.

The offended whitehead

These obstinate blemishes like to be left alone to consolidate and become more unsightly. They hate being touched, and can often be made to go away if very, very gently and persistently rubbed with the tip of a finger-nail. Do NOT scratch. A few seconds every day will do, and one day your unwelcome whitehead may be seen to have taken itself off in a huff.

Lip sealing

A very old granny told me that she used to heal cracked lips (her own, I hope) with ear wax. She said it worked like magic. It would need to!

Eggshells

Mother would collect eggshells from the breakfast table and crush them up, not to prevent witches from using them as boats, but for use as nail strengtheners. She put a small mound of the crushed shells into the palm of one hand and bunched the fingertips of the other into this, using a grinding action. Then of course she changed hands. Her tendency to soft nails was very much lessened by this economical treatment.

Nature's toothpowder

Juniper leaves and twigs picked when the sap is full, dried in a warm place, then put in a suitably large tin in which they may be set on fire, make a fine ash that is wonderful for cleaning the teeth. It whitens them and prevents decay. Also good for the treatment of gum ulcers.

Orange aid

A 19th century cure for a cold was to pare the rind of an orange very finely into short strips, roll them up inside out, and place one roll in each nostril. If one couldn't breathe through the nose anyway, it was probably safe to block the nose in this way!

Night cough

Glycerine and claret in equal parts as a dispeller of the tickle that keeps one coughing at night is something that must surely make Bacchus weep. But one will try anything to induce a peaceful sleep.

Advice to intrepids

If the whiff of bad drains, or non drains, makes one fearful of terrible infections, it is a simple and wise precaution to suck a sulphur tablet. I did this when walking through some of Calcutta's less savoury districts and was attacked by no germs.

Insomnia

One should try to catch this unawares, so to speak. It can sometimes be done by throwing off the bedclothes and remaining uncovered until you feel chilly. Then the act of snuggling back under the clothes with relief can chase away the tenseness that was keeping you awake. Pneumonia may take the place of insomnia if one's timing is not well calculated!

Night cramp

The popular remedy for this distressing ailment (mentioned in my previous book), consisting of putting wine corks in the bed, may be further improved by the addition of a simple pin magnet to this immunity kit.

World's best shampoo

According to what my dear Mrs Lavender writes in her Herbal Book of yesteryear, this is egg and borax. Wet the head, rub in the yolk only of a fresh egg until it lathers, and continue massaging. Rinse in warm water into which a heaped teaspoonful of borax has been dissolved to each quart.

Bald statement

Green leaves of Jerusalem artichokes stewed with a little water for three hours will produce a liquid said to cure baldness if applied to the scalp two or three times a week. The mixture should *not* be strained before use.

Grey hair

I used to keep away when Grandmother applied her favourite lotion to darken her greying hair, because I hate the smell of sage. But a handful of this herb, fresh or dried, covered with half a pint of boiling water with a teaspoon of borax added, allowed to get cold, does make an excellent cover up. It should be applied lightly to the hair with a brush or sponge.

OUT
AND
ABOUT

Safe seat

My very resourceful friend came to visit me on her
bicycle. Before coming indoors she asked me for some
silver foil. This she carefully moulded over the saddle.
Having looked at the sky she expected rain, and this
was her way of ensuring a dry seat.

Snow

A plastic dustpan carried in the car serves as a scoop for the fast removal of snow from a car that has become blanketed. The plastic edge causes no scratching of the coachwork.

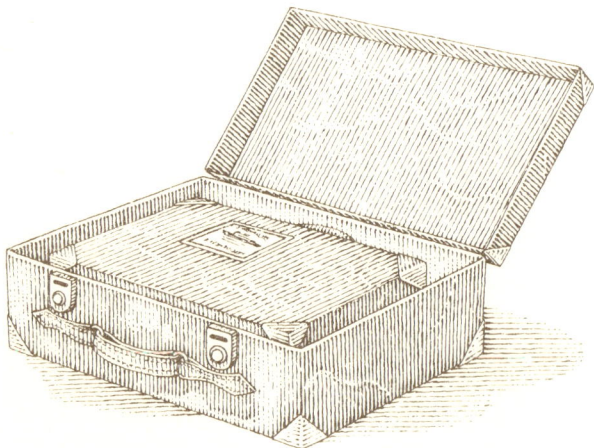

The disappearing suitcase

Mother always managed to start off on holiday with one suitcase in her hand and return with two. She would have packed one case and then put it inside a slightly larger one. In this way she had a container in which to bring back all the souvenirs and presents for the family.

Cool it

When travelling to a hot clime, take the precaution of packing swim things and a robe in your hand luggage so that on arrival at the hotel, where it is more than likely your room will not be ready, you can leave your big luggage with the hall porter while you head for a refreshing dip in the pool. Much wiser than sitting in the lounge and fuming.

Foldaway

A gentleman's gentleman was kind enough to give me a lesson in packing, and I give below some of the methods he employed and which I now always adopt:

Never mix shoes with other clothes. They should travel in a separate bag.

Trousers must lie at the bottom of case. Place a rolled vest or suchlike inside the fold-over.

Lay shirts, jerseys, blouses, dresses, flat on top of each other in types. Fold them as one, across or lengthways to fit case, with a rolled-up item inside the top fold. Thus each garment protects another.

And never pack 'his' and 'hers' in separate cases. They sometimes go off on separate planes and get lost. Always mix the contents.

Switch off

Before packing an electric torch in your luggage, stick adhesive tape over the switch to make sure that it doesn't get turned on by accident. This prevents the dreadful frustration of negotiating dark hotel corridors in the middle of the night because a battery has wasted its energy inside a suitcase.

Open wide

The afternoon appointment with my dentist had come round with unwelcome speed, and I also had a lunch date for the same day. I would have to take my toothbrush and somehow manage to use it in order not to present the dentist with captive particles of meat fibre or delectable hazelnuts. But the bottom of my handbag is not all that hygienic. Remembering my friend who covers her bicycle saddle with silver foil, I did the same with the head of my brush. Top marks from the dentist for a well kept mouth were my reward for ingenuity.

Balcony scene

To obtain front row seats in a theatre circle is usually regarded as a bit of luck. But what a disappointment when a brass guard rail obstructs the view of the stage. To sit in the second row, above the rail's obstruction, brings another hazard: people in the first row lean forward in order to peer over the balcony front, thus effectively blocking one's view. Experience has proved that the best balcony seat for good viewing is in the third row, where one rises above the nuisances here mentioned.

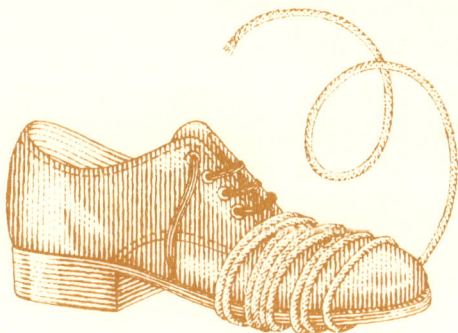

Anti-skid

It is possible to walk much more safely on icy pavements if thick string is first of all wound round and round one's shoes after they have been put on. In effect one obtains a rope sole.

The moving archangel

The Archangel Michael is the instigator of change and new impulse. For this reason the Michaelmas Quarter is the busiest time of the year for removal firms. Remembering this, it is well to give plenty of notice if one has to move house in this period, or to postpone the move into the next Quarter.

Look, no corkscrew!

When it looks like being a dry picnic because someone's forgotten to pack the corkscrew, do not despair. If you have a book handy, simply hit the bottom of the bottle repeatedly and sharply until the cork is seen to rise gradually from its seat. A dozen or more blows may be needed. It goes without saying that a stone would be disastrous to use, but sufficiently padded it might serve. A rubber soled shoe would be much better.

LOOKING
AT
FOOD

Sweet advice

We took Mother out to dinner and asked her to choose
the appetisers. Surely she would have her favourite egg
mayonnaise? 'Let me have a look at the sweet trolley,'
she commanded. She examined it thoughtfully before
saying, 'Yes, I *will* have the egg mayonnaise.' 'But why
did you have to look at the sweets?' I asked. 'Because,
my dears, if there are meringues and they are craggy
and slightly beige they are home-made. Therefore
there are egg yolks left over, and one may pretty
safely presume that the mayonnaise will be home-
made.'

Egg lore

It used to be considered unlucky to carry eggs in or
out of the house after dark. Sailors were superstitious
about even mentioning them by name at sea, and eggs
sold on board meant bad luck. I believe that the
superstitions concerning eggs stem from the truly
awful experience of encountering a bad one. Remember
Belloc's missionary, or the hapless curate? The sul-
phurous stink would in the past have spoken of the

regions of Hell. So precautions like the following have been evolved over the years:

Test large end of an egg with tip of the tongue. If it feels warm it is new. If cold, not so new.

Turn eggs in store at least once a week. They will remain fresh for months.

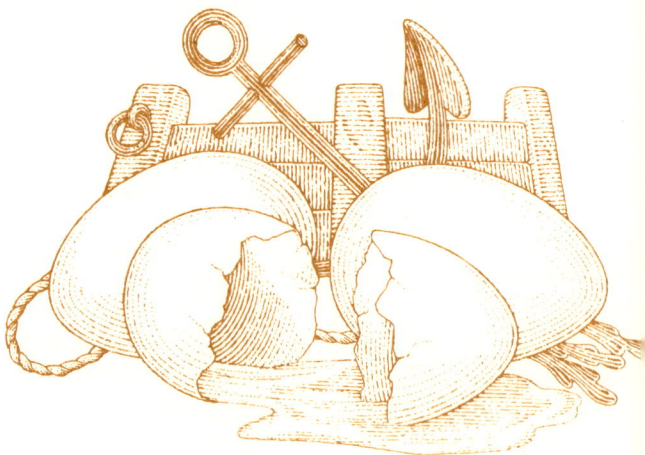

Nostalgia

Why were the fried eggs of my childhood so delicious? Because they were dropped into very hot butter to acquire lacy crisp edges and the heat turned low after a few moments. A sprinkle of salt over the yolks just before the end of cooking time also made all the difference.

Onion speed

When just the juice of an onion is needed for a recipe, this can be quickly obtained by squeezing a halved onion on a lemon squeezer. A glass one is best since it won't retain the flavour.

Peeling an onion is often a slow and fidgety job. If there is no need for fine dice – for which there is a special method of cutting – the peeling process is certainly speeded up if the first cut is made through the onion's equator, so to speak, and not from north to south.

Writing in syrup

I was often late for school because I took so long over my porridge. I just had to write my name with the syrup as it trickled from the spoon. In exasperation Mother found a way of speeding matters up. She steeped my spoon first of all in a cup of hot tea, then into the syrup. The syrup flowed much more quickly from the hot spoon – but it wasn't such fun.

Diminished fortune

Mr Colman is supposed to have made his fortune from the mustard that people left on their plates or that dried up in little pots. He might not have been so fortunate if his customers had always added some salt when mixing the mustard powder with water. This prevents it from drying out.

Fire!

We had a family friend who loved everything very hot. He was always burning his tongue on roast potatoes. But as he had a cure for such an accident he didn't really mind. He would dip his tongue into an eggcup of vinegar to ease the pain.

Horseradish sauce, lots of it, was another addiction, and he had a cure for a mouth that felt as if it was going to burst into flames. A slice of fresh bread held over the nose and mouth and breathed through would cool everything down. Very likely this would help with fiery curry also.

Ginger

Take fresh ginger, peel, dice, and steep in sherry. Cork. The sherry takes on the flavour of the ginger, which is good for flavouring use; but the ginger pieces retain their own flavour and do not absorb that of the sherry. They are moist and always ready for use.

Fanny's dumplings

Fanny was a Czech, and no one knows more about dumplings than they do. I watched her as she worked in her kitchen, and was surprised to note that she wet her hands with cold water before shaping the dough into balls. I'd always been taught to flour my hands. But now I do as Fanny did, because in every way it is more efficient. The hands do not get clammed up with sticky flour.

Chop chop

In France parsley is chopped in a bowl with scissors pointing downward.

In England it is prepared for decorative use by being roughly chopped, piled into centre of a fine cloth, twisted into a tight bundle that is held under a fast-running tap. The bundle is then opened and the parsley spread to dry on kitchen paper. Afterwards it is wrapped in fresh paper and stored in the fridge for later use. It remains bright green for weeks and becomes very finely crumbled – just right for topping off dishes.

In my kitchen, when parsley is used for its high Vitamin C content as soon after picking as possible, it is bunched tightly with the fingers on a board and cut closely across in fine slicing movements. Fingernails are safe provided they are kept pointing downward at absolute right-angles to the board.

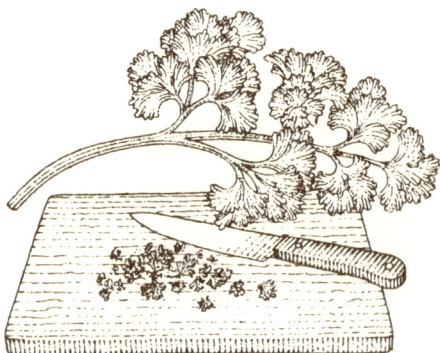

Another day

A greedy young visitor came to lunch one day and in the middle of his trifle warned, 'Don't anyone have any more because I shall be wanting it.' Apart from being shocked, Mother had her own views about second helpings. She hated to give them. Her first helpings were always very generous, and she would contrive to leave something in the serving dish that got spirited away rather quickly back to the kitchen. She regarded a left-over as something that with the aid of imagination and certain additions could become the basis for tomorrow's lunch. 'Think of tomorrow, and don't force that last scrap on people who've already eaten far too much.' With fridges to keep left-overs overnight there seems to be no harm and a great deal of economic sense in this advice.

Roast chicken

It sometimes happens that an otherwise perfectly roasted bird has the inside part of the legs still unpleasantly pink and undercooked. This is due to tight trussing which prevents the heat from getting into these recesses. The bird may quite safely be cooked without any string to hold it together if it is first placed on one side for twenty minutes' cooking, turned onto its other side for a similar period, and then finally onto its back for the remainder of the cooking time. Juices flow into the legs to keep them moist during the first two stages, and then the heat can get at the insides of them during the last stage. There is no need to fear that the bird will spring about in the pan if not laced up like an Edwardian lady.

Butter softener

Pour boiling water into a pudding basin. Leave to heat through. Empty it and invert over a hard slab of butter. This will give something nice and workable and never the oily mess that other fast measures often produce.

Coal black fresh

It is nutritionally not a good thing to prepare vegetables far in advance and leave them soaking in water. But sometimes expediency is more important and potatoes have to be peeled the night before they are needed. The trouble is that they tend to discolour. Prevent this by putting a small lump of coal in the water they are to soak in. Next day they will look as fresh as if newly peeled.

The above advice was new to me, but I did know that a limp lettuce can be crisped by soaking in water with a piece of coal.

HOMEWORK

Wicker and bamboo

Living rooms now tend to look like garden bowers with the present craze for cane furniture. This is best dusted in all its nooks and crannies with an artist's long paint-brush. When this furniture becomes dirty, a shampoo with salt and water applied with a soft brush will bring it up like new. But at all times one should treat the bindings with gentleness. Once they start to unravel there is endless trouble.

Dirty wood

The top rails of dining chairs, fronts of drawers, bannister rails, sometimes acquire hard black streaks from constant handling in grimy atmospheres. These marks can get beyond responding to ordinary polishing, but may be removed by rubbing with the following mixture:

1 part turpentine

1 part vinegar

Enough powdered starch to make a paste.

The acky rag

My window cleaner tucked his blackened leather into the belt of his trousers and prepared for a chat. Sticking to business, I asked him about cleaning methods. He told me that in the past, when they had a large and dirty building to cope with for the first time, they used an acky rag. 'Brings the windows up lovely and sparkling. But you can never use water on them again.' Such a rag is a piece of scrim dipped in paraffin and baked in the oven. The drawback is that dirt gets attracted to the slightly greasy surface left by the rag. So never employ a window cleaner who smells of paraffin.

Island shine

The Maltese use cotton tops of stockings for polishing silver. They boil them in a little milk, and the result is similar to commercially impregnated cloths that rub up silver without polish. Cotton stocking tops do not abound in many households now, but the stuff we used to call locknit is what is needed.

Brassed off

One need never do another messy polishing job on brass if the following advice is taken. Once the brass is in tip-top shine by the old method, it can be kept that way by a daily dusting with a duster that has been previously warmed between the hands.

De-scaling

A handful of ordinary soda in boiling water will remove tannin coating from inside metal teapots when allowed to steep for a few hours. Particularly useful for silver pots.

Branded denture cleaners make excellent de-scaling agents when shower heads become so clogged they only offer trickles instead of jets.

Anti-splash

Some pieces of advice seem too obvious to be voiced, but I am ever grateful for Mother's warning to remove the unused kettle from the top of the stove when doing other cooking, especially frying. It must have saved me lots of time trying to shine up my kettle and remove grease splashes from it.

Venetian glass

'My heart grows large when I meet an English lady,' declared the Venetian shop owner, making me feel like Katherine Hepburn. So I bought the six glasses I couldn't afford. I got a bonus, though. He told me how to care for them: Wash in hot soapy water, rinse in warm water with vinegar added. He omitted to mention the quantity, but two tablespoonfuls in an average bowl does very nicely.

The good cooker

I had a friend who took on a job as a door-to-door salesman for gas cookers. He had a hard job trying to persuade a woman to exchange an old black stove for a shining white one. Reluctantly she admitted a hankering for one with 'that new virtuous enamel'. Having got it she could have kept it clean by treating stains with one tablespoonful of paraffin mixed with two of salt, and rinsing off with hot water and soda.

Tub sense

It had seemed the height of fussiness when I noted someone not only rinsing out the bath but also drying it. When it was pointed out that this prevented those scaly patches near the outlet I was impressed. If a bath is rinsed and left, in time all those little drops on the side slide down to collect in small pools, and evaporation leaves a deposit round the edges.

Gloves

Fabric gloves should always be worn when under-taking the cleaning of chandeliers. Bare fingers will leave a greasy film on the crystal.

Long fingernails go through the tips of rubber gloves in no time at all. Much longer wear will result if fabric gloves are worn inside the rubber ones.

Pewter

Wood ash mixed to a paste with water makes a good cleanser for pewter, and it will help to maintain the correct dull sheen.

Sick bed

An adjustable ironing board can make a useful bed table for a child who has to be kept amused during a spell in bed. It will stretch across the bed and hold the various jigsaws and other distractions.

Carpet first aid

Hitler used to get down and bite his carpets. Mother was more civilised and used a knife and fork! It happened this way: a very sticky piece of chocolate cake was trodden into her carpet by a young visitor. Some-one got down at once and began to scrape with the edge of a knife. 'Now use a fork,' Mother instructed, and she showed how the prongs would lift out particles of the mess that remained embedded by the knife treatment, and at the same time raise up the pile again.

If a visiting dog commits an indiscretion on the carpet because he couldn't communicate his needs, mop

47

up and wash with soda water and small brush. Rinse and rub dry. The dog may be invited again.

Cigarette burns on carpets can be effectively treated by being rubbed with the edge of a silver coin.

Cutting the cost

Cut Brillo pads in half with scissors. Two smaller fresh pads are better than a large one kept until it rusts and disintegrates.

Long time no see

When my short-sighted friend dropped one of her contact lenses yet again, and this time onto a shaggy rug, I prepared to go down on my knees to make a Sherlock Holmes search. 'No need for that,' she said, and went to fetch her vacuum cleaner. This horrified me, until I saw that she was pulling a nylon stocking over the end of the hose attachment. She then methodically vacuumed the rug, and presently the minute glass disc was found sucked up and held against the stocking mesh.

CLOTH
SENSE

Rapunzel action

Father tore his jacket sleeve just as he was dashing off to work. Quick as a flash Mother got a needle, pulled a long hair out of her head, and quite firmly and invisibly stitched down the edges of the tear with this seemingly fragile thread. I was dubious about the possibility of it holding, but as usual Mother was imaginatively right – the darn lasted not just for the day but for several weeks, and then a professional invisible mender took over.

Press studs

The correct way to sew these onto a garment is for the thinner section (with the knob) to be attached to the upper edge of the opening. This makes for less stress on the cloth during use.

Sleeve lengthening

Provided there is a fairly deep hem at the wrist, it makes a neater job of lengthening a sleeve to cut the lining near the elbow and to insert a strip of lining there. Then the hem at the wrist can be lowered and pressed to give the extra length provided by the insertion. The original tidy stitching of the hem is thus preserved.

Let down

For little girls who don't go around looking like miniature boilermen, here is a hint to bear in mind when hanging out their dresses to dry in the sun. Peg them inside out so that the hem turn-backs fade a little to keep up with the general fading of the right side. When lengthening has to take place there is very much less difference in colour.

Tender loving care

I was shocked when I first undressed my new baby and saw the marks on his tender skin that had been made by the lovingly knitted vest. Done in stocking stitch, and made up as usual with the smooth side outwards and seams on the inside, of course it had marked the baby. After that I always put the vest on him inside out for his comfort. In fact, I wish that all underwear were made up in this way, particularly foundation garments.

Silks and laces

These are very much back in vogue after being banned both by their cost and our involvement with easy-care materials. Here is a little advice for those unfamiliar with these delicate items:

A little methylated spirit added to the rinsing water will preserve the sheen of silk. It should be ironed hot.

Lace can be stiffened after washing by soaking in sugar water made up in the proportion of two lumps to a pint of water. Clean old lace by sprinkling it with powdered magnesia and leaving for a few days before shaking it out. The powder will have absorbed much of the dirt.

Rust

Rust marks on material are generally very difficult to remove, partly because they are not discovered when fresh. Proprietary brands of rust remover work well on strong material but should never be employed on delicate stuff. One can try sprinkling on salt and rubbing with a cut lemon, as long as this method is employed with the greatest delicacy.

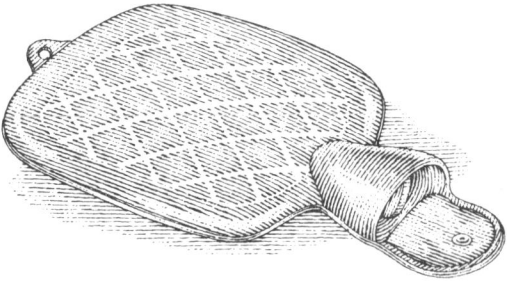

Storing rubber

Never put your swim cap away in a drawer for next summer without stuffing it with paper or a small rolled-up garment. Failure to do this will often result in the rubber surfaces sticking together and ruining the cap.

Hot water bottles, for the same reason, should be blown into as if they were balloons and stoppered before storing.

Colour from elderberry

This tree is a good friend to those who go in for natural home dyeing. The leaves provide green, the berries purple, and the flowers yellow.

Saving your skin

Seat belts are a safety must. There is no doubt about that; but undoubtedly they do wear out the fronts of coats and jackets. A scarf can be slipped underneath to take the rub. But a passenger with a fur coat should take this off before getting into the car. After fastening the belt, the arms can be slipped into the sleeves and the fur worn back to front on top of the belt. Or, simpler still, the coat can be used as a luxurious knee rug.

Fitted sheets

'You've got something big to remember,' I said, as I watched Mother tying knots in a sheet. It turned out that she was converting a flat sheet into a fitted bottom sheet by tying a knot in each corner. The knots can be undone later to make laundering easier.

Static

Sharing a hotel room with another woman, I was so maddened by the slowness with which she undressed that I had to comment. She said that with so many man-made fibres in our garments, static electricity was increased if they were drawn sharply across each other. She demonstrated, and the sparks flew in the darkness. Next time such charged clothes are worn they behave like magnets and cling most uncomfortably. So now I always peel skirts off very slowly when worn over nylon slips or tights.

Slippery customer

I used to visit an old lady who did nothing all day but sit in a chair and eat biscuits between meals. To keep her looking spick and span her daughter kept her in taffeta dresses. Crumbs slip off this kind of material very easily, and it never looks dusty. In cold weather it was quite easy for Gran to wear something warm and woolly underneath.

GROWING
POINTS

Honeysuckle air

The cottage was idyllic with honeysuckle growing by the door. But the owner was always threatening to uproot it because, after the weeks of scented flowering, blackfly infested it as the seed began to form. Oddly, another honeysuckle of the same type that was trained up a fir tree, remained unvisited by this pest. A scientific gardener explained that it was the lack of ventilation for the plant that grew up the wall that made a haven for the fly. The one growing round the tree trunk had plenty of wind blowing through and this made it inhospitable.

Soil test

Germination failure is often caused by sowing seed in ground that is too cold. An old American test is to insert an iron poker into the ground for a minute or so. Then, when it is lifted out and laid against the cheek, if it feels no more than cool, the time is right for sowing. If really cold, give the sun more time to warm the ground.

Leeks

If you are made to try a glass of Guinness and have a job getting it down, you can do a leek a good turn by emptying the stuff round it. In the North, where they go in for leek-growing competitions, this is one of the ingredients used to stimulate growth. Soot is another.

Tomatoes, good and bad

Old gardeners uproot tomato plants at the end of the season and hang them on boughs of fruit trees to wither. This prevents diseases and blight. Sometimes they burn the old plants under apple trees so that the smoke rising among the branches will destroy insects and blight.

Anyone prone to attacks of gout should never eat tomatoes.

Yarrow

At the trial of Elspeth Reoch for witchcraft it was claimed that she could cure distempers by resting on her right knee whilst pulling the herb called *malefour* betwixt her mid-finger and thumb and chanting obscenities. Milfoil is another name for yarrow. One can't help wishing that as distemper is not a term for a precise illness known today, it would have been more interesting to know what the obscenities were!

Yarrow, however, is an excellent and fast activator on the compost heap. Three or four leaves finely chopped and distributed among the layers cause the heap to sink quite dramatically.

Gravity feed

Having to site my vegetable patch in a corner and just in front of the compost heaps seemed at first to be unsatisfactory. In addition, the ground was slightly sloping. Now I realise that there is an automatic drainage feed from the compost right across the plot, which saves quite a lot of work forking in fertilisers. In future I shall seek similar sites.

Written out

Used-up, transparent biro pens make unobtrusive supports for pot plants.

Pampered grass

I was surprised when Mother asked to borrow my hairspray, because she likes her hair to be fluffy and free. But I found her spraying the plumes of pampas grass she had brought indoors for decoration. This was a procedure to prevent the seeds and fluff from flying off all over the room.

Flower arrangers, using small strands from a plume, dip them in glycerine, which also makes them supple and silvery.

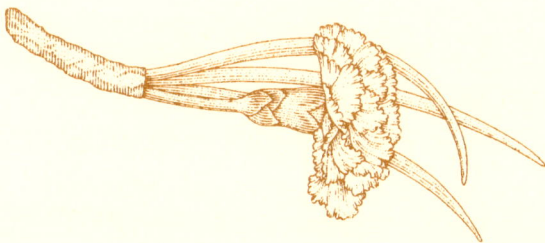

Buttonhole reviver

Those tired and tortured buttonholes of carnation or rose that we bring back from weddings can be perked up and kept fresh for a long time (some say up to six weeks) if placed in a small vase filled half with water and half old-fashioned fizzy lemonade.

Lavender

After the dainty lavender bags have been made up for the next church bazaar, keep the stripped stalks and pack into old stockings. They smell as strongly as the flowers, and will serve for the dark linen cupboard shelves.

Slipped shoulders

Forget about knee guards by sewing old shoulder pads inside your gardening trousers.

Watering

Mother sent me to fetch ice cubes from the fridge, but she didn't add them to her drink. She let them melt and get to room temperature and used this to water her house plants – which always look wonderful. I also know someone who uses water from the fish tank for their plants.

Drainage

Keep all the cracked nutshells from Christmas nibblings for use as lightweight drainage material for hanging pot plants. Much kinder on the ceiling hook than broken crocks.

Old sponges, of whatever material, can be cut to shape and placed at the bottom of flower pots, under the soil. They retain water for the roots and let the rest drain out of the hole.

Sunflowers

If these are planted against the walls of a house suffering from rising damp, the condition will be cured without the expense of modern scientific methods. At least, so my Dutch friend tells me, claiming that areas of marshland have been made usable by planting sunflowers lavishly on them.

Hide-and-seek

It is presumably a question of aesthetics that makes manufacturers of garden tools paint the handles a soupy green. Once laid aside in the garden a trowel can vanish for days as it lies camouflaged in the grass. One should get a pot of red paint and spend a winter afternoon decorating all the handles in the garden shed.

INDEX